EXPLORING SOCIAL INJUSTICE
INJUSTICE AGAINST WOMEN

by Tammy Gagne

BrightPoint Press

San Diego, CA

© 2023 BrightPoint Press
an imprint of ReferencePoint Press, Inc.
Printed in the United States

For more information, contact:
BrightPoint Press
PO Box 27779
San Diego, CA 92198
www.BrightPointPress.com

ALL RIGHTS RESERVED.

No part of this work covered by the copyright hereon may be reproduced or used in any form or by any means—graphic, electronic, or mechanical, including photocopying, recording, taping, web distribution, or information storage retrieval systems—without the written permission of the publisher.

Content Consultant: Pamela Aronson, PhD; Professor of Sociology and Affiliate in Women's and Gender Studies, University of Michigan–Dearborn

LIBRARY OF CONGRESS CATALOGING-IN-PUBLICATION DATA

Name: Gagne, Tammy, author.
Title: Injustice against women / by Tammy Gagne.
Description: San Diego, CA: BrightPoint Press, [2023] | Series: Exploring social injustice | Includes bibliographical references and index. | Audience: Grades 10–12
Identifiers: ISBN 9781678203986 (hardcover) | ISBN 9781678203993 (eBook)
The complete Library of Congress record is available at www.loc.gov.

CONTENTS

AT A GLANCE	4
INTRODUCTION	6
REFUSING TO BE SILENCED	
CHAPTER ONE	12
THE HISTORY OF INJUSTICE AGAINST WOMEN	
CHAPTER TWO	24
INJUSTICE AGAINST WOMEN TODAY	
CHAPTER THREE	36
KEY MOMENTS IN FIGHTING INJUSTICE AGAINST WOMEN	
CHAPTER FOUR	46
ENDING INJUSTICE AGAINST WOMEN	
Glossary	58
Source Notes	59
For Further Research	60
Index	62
Image Credits	63
About the Author	64

AT A GLANCE

- The United States has a history of injustices against women. For much of the country's history, US women were not allowed to vote, own property, or serve on juries.

- The Nineteenth Amendment gave women the right to vote. It was added to the US Constitution in 1920.

- An extremist group called the Taliban regained control of Afghanistan in 2021. Historically, the group has limited women's rights. It reduced educational and work opportunities for women again after retaking power.

- Women in the United States make 82 cents for every dollar that men earn. This is known as the gender pay gap.

- In the case *Roe v. Wade*, the US Supreme Court protected a woman's choice to get an abortion.

- Geraldine Ferraro became the first woman nominated for US vice president in 1984. Kamala Harris became the first woman to serve in the position in 2021.

- In 2017, women came forward and accused movie producer Harvey Weinstein of sexual harassment. This sparked the #MeToo movement. Many women began to talk about harassment and assault.

- Young girls can be forced into arranged marriages in some countries. This can limit their educations. They may be forced into abusive relationships.

INTRODUCTION

REFUSING TO BE SILENCED

Malala Yousafzai was born in Pakistan. She started a blog in 2009. She was just twelve years old. An extremist group called the Taliban controlled part of the country. Malala wrote about what it was like to live under its rule. The Taliban did not want girls to be educated. The group destroyed more than 400 schools to prevent girls from attending.

But Malala kept going to school. She started giving speeches about the injustices girls faced under the Taliban. She talked

Malala Yousafzai published a book in 2013 about her fight for girls' education.

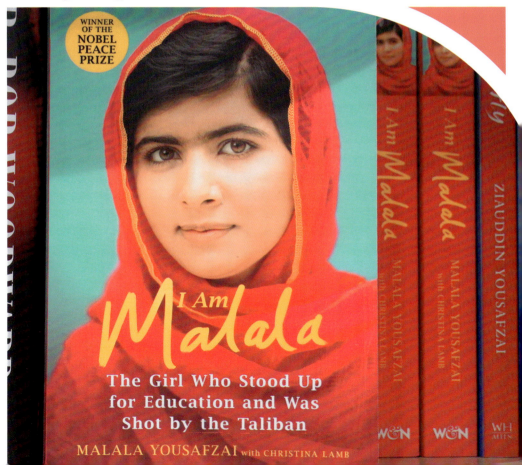

Many Afghan women fled the country after the Taliban regained control of Afghanistan in 2021.

about the importance of education. Malala was returning home from school in 2012. Taliban members stopped the bus. They wanted to stop Malala from sharing her story. They shot Malala. But she survived. She would not let the Taliban silence her. She wrote a book about the experience after she recovered. She also launched the Malala Fund. This charity raises money for girls' education.

Malala won the Nobel Peace Prize in 2014. As of 2021, she was the youngest person to receive the award. She graduated from Oxford University in the United Kingdom in 2020. The Malala Fund had raised more than $22 million by 2022. Malala continues to be a role model for girls and women everywhere.

Voting is one way to have one's voice represented in government.

WHAT ARE INJUSTICES AGAINST WOMEN?

Injustices against women happen worldwide. Some governments do not give women the right to vote. Women do not have a say in decisions that affect their lives. Companies do not always pay women fairly.

One way to fight injustice is through education. This raises awareness. People can speak out against injustice. They can work toward changes in government. They can support laws that give women equal opportunities.

1
THE HISTORY OF INJUSTICE AGAINST WOMEN

An early example of injustice against women can be seen in ancient Roman society. In the first century CE, Roman men had complete authority over women. Men were allowed to kill their wives and daughters if the women caused shame to the household. Roman girls and women could receive only a basic education. Many received no education at all. Most women were not allowed to own property. Girls had to obey their fathers. Husbands made decisions for their wives.

Traditional gender roles in ancient Roman society severely limited opportunities for women.

The Continental Congress included leaders that shaped the US government. All the members were male.

INJUSTICE IN AMERICA

Injustices against women can be seen in US history. British colonies in America had laws that limited women's rights in the 1700s. Women were not allowed to own property.

The colonies fought for independence in the Revolutionary War (1775–1783). Lawmakers began to form a new government. But women were not allowed to participate. The New York State Constitution was created in 1777. It defined voters as male inhabitants. Other colonies created similar laws. Women were not able to vote for more than 100 years. Voting is one way for one's voice to be heard. Voters can elect officials who have similar beliefs

A group of female suffragists gathered in Washington, DC, in 1888.

to them. Then the officials can help create changes that voters want.

Hundreds of women and men gathered in Seneca Falls, New York, in 1848. They met to discuss women's rights. They wanted to give women the right to vote.

This meeting was a major event in the women's **suffrage** movement.

Elizabeth Cady Stanton fought for women's suffrage. Other suffragists included Susan B. Anthony and Lucretia Mott. They traveled around the country. They gave speeches about women's

BLACK SUFFRAGISTS

White women did not always include Black suffragists. In 1913, the National American Woman Suffrage Association marched on Washington, DC. Leaders of the organization forced Black women to walk at the end of the parade. Ida B. Wells-Barnett refused. The Black journalist walked alongside other women representing Illinois. They stood together in the fight for equal suffrage for all.

suffrage. Stanton and Anthony published a newspaper about the cause. It was called *The Revolution*.

The Nineteenth Amendment was added to the US Constitution in 1920. This amendment made it possible for women to vote. But many women still could not vote due to other factors, such as race. For example, some states used voting taxes to stop Black Americans from voting. Many were unable to pay the fee.

Women also could not be part of a **jury** for much of US history. A jury is made up of a group of citizens. It decides

A fair jury includes community members of different ages and ethnicities.

whether a person is guilty of a crime. The US Constitution states that people have the right to a fair trial by jury. A fair jury today includes people of different backgrounds. This means including people of different genders and races.

Having an all-male jury can lead to **bias**. In 1898, Utah became the first state to allow women to serve on juries. As recently as 1961, the US Supreme Court ruled that it was not necessary to include women on a jury. It took until 1973 for all fifty states to allow women to appear on a jury.

A STEP FORWARD AND A STEP BACK

Many American men fought overseas during World War II (1939–1945). Women entered the paid workforce in large numbers while men were at war. They manufactured supplies. Some women gave up their jobs after the war. But employers fired many women. The jobs were given to returning soldiers.

The Supreme Court reversed its ruling in 1974. It decided that men and women were both needed for a fair jury.

THE EQUAL RIGHTS AMENDMENT

Women's rights activists began working toward another goal. Crystal Eastman and Alice Paul drafted the Lucretia Mott Amendment. People later called it the Equal Rights Amendment (ERA). The ERA stated that, "Men and women shall have equal rights throughout the United States and every place subject to its jurisdiction."[1] The amendment would

Alice Paul sews a suffrage flag. Paul organized protests and parades in support of women's suffrage.

help end **discrimination** based on sex. Supporters wanted it to be added to the US Constitution.

Congress saw the first draft of the ERA in 1923. But the ERA did not gain serious attention until the 1970s. It passed through Congress in 1972. The next step was for the states to approve it. An amendment needs to be approved by thirty-eight states. Otherwise it cannot be added to the US Constitution. Only thirty-three states had approved the ERA by the end of 1974.

The status of the ERA was still being debated into the 2020s. Virginia approved the ERA in 2020. It was the thirty-eighth state to do so. But opponents of the ERA decided that the deadline to vote on the bill had passed.

2
INJUSTICE AGAINST WOMEN TODAY

There are many examples of injustice against women in the world today. One can be seen in Afghanistan. A group called the Taliban runs the country. The Taliban has an extreme interpretation of Islam. The group has used its beliefs to justify discrimination against women.

A US invasion in 2001 removed it from power. But the Taliban regained control of Afghanistan in August 2021. Many people worried what this would mean for Afghan

The rights of women and girls in Afghanistan are threatened under Taliban rule.

Some Muslim women choose to wear a hijab as a symbol of their faith.

women and girls. The Taliban claimed it would not discriminate against women. But it shut down a government department that promoted women's rights. It also created laws that threatened women's rights.

The Taliban discriminates against women in many ways. Under Taliban rule, men do not have clothing restrictions. But the Taliban required all women to wear burqas from 1996 to 2001. A burqa is a large veil that covers a woman's head, face, and body. Some Muslim women choose to wear burqas or other religious coverings. They view these coverings as symbols of their culture and faith. Some women have reported that Taliban soldiers have tried to force them to wear burqas. Women do not have a choice about how to express their religious beliefs.

The Taliban restricted job opportunities for women. The city of Kabul prevented female government employees from working in October 2021. Women were not allowed to appear on television.

At first, the Taliban allowed some women to attend universities. But their freedoms

KEEPING WOMEN FROM WORKING

Women do not have the right to work in eighteen countries. These countries have laws that allow men to decide whether their wives can work. More than one hundred countries have laws that prevent women from working certain jobs. These laws give men financial power over their wives.

were limited. They could not sit next to or even be seen by male students. By 2022, the Taliban had closed many girls' schools.

Taliban rule also restricted travel. Women could not travel more than 45 miles (72 km) from home without a male relative. Drivers could not pick up women without veils.

THE GENDER PAY GAP

Women are up to five times more likely than men to work a part-time job. These positions are typically low paying. Women are often the caregivers in their households. They may be forced into part-time jobs so they have time for their children. Men are more likely to hold high-paying positions than women are. In 2021, 92 percent of the chief executive officers of top US companies were male.

Women have earned less money than men throughout history. On average, US women earned 82 cents for every dollar that men earned in 2021. Women of color earned even less. This difference in pay is called the gender pay gap.

Women earn less than men even when doing the same jobs. President John F. Kennedy signed the Equal Pay Act into law

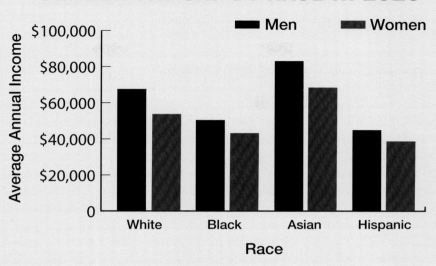

The gender pay gap exists across all races. Women of all races earn less than their male counterparts.

in 1963. It promised equal pay for the same work regardless of gender, race, or religion. But pay discrimination continues today.

In a 2017 survey, 42 percent of US women reported facing gender discrimination at work. Dr. Bryan Robinson is an author and journalist. He talked about workplace discrimination. He said, "It's . . . not unusual for women to receive less pay, fewer benefits, fewer opportunities, or to be passed up for jobs or promotions for which they are well qualified." [2]

Employers may judge female workers unfairly. They may describe a confident man as being a leader. But they may describe a woman who behaves the same way as being bossy. It can be challenging for women to enter the workforce. Gender discrimination is illegal. But companies may be more willing to hire men.

HUMAN TRAFFICKING

Human traffickers kidnap victims. They sell people into slavery. Victims of human

DOMESTIC ABUSE

Domestic abuse is abuse that comes from a significant other. It can be physical or emotional. Women are more likely to experience this abuse than men are. More than 640 million women over the age of fifteen have experienced violence from their partners. Victims of domestic abuse can call the National Domestic Abuse Hotline. They can visit the hotline's website. It offers tools and support for those who have experienced domestic violence.

Members and supporters of the A21 Campaign work to end human trafficking and other forms of slavery.

trafficking may be forced to work in unsafe conditions. They may be sold into abusive relationships. About 80 percent of trafficking victims are women and children. Human traffickers trick people with promises of a better life. Many victims are poor. Worldwide, women are more likely to live in poverty than men are. They may not have equal job opportunities. Inequalities make them vulnerable to trafficking.

Margeaux Gray was sold into human trafficking as a child. She escaped. Gray is now the president of the Mentari Human Trafficking Survivor Empowerment Program. This organization helps victims of human trafficking. Gray talked about justice. "I speak out so that other victims and survivors know that they are not alone," she said. "There is help, and there is hope."[3]

3
KEY MOMENTS IN FIGHTING INJUSTICE AGAINST WOMEN

The women's suffrage moment succeeded. The Nineteenth Amendment was added to the Constitution on August 18, 1920. But more work was needed. People continue to fight for gender equality.

Donald Trump ran for president in 2016. A video leaked during his campaign. In it, he talked about assaulting women because he is powerful. Republicans and Democrats criticized Trump's behavior. Trump won the

Hundreds of thousands of women protested in Washington, DC, as part of the Women's March in 2017.

presidential election. Women gathered in Washington, DC, in January 2017 on the day Trump took office. They joined together for the Women's March. The women wanted to make sure the new president would not ignore women's rights. The Women's March was one of the largest single-day protests in US history. More than 4 million people took part.

ROE V. WADE

In 1973, the US Supreme Court made a ruling in the case *Roe v. Wade*. It declared that women have a right to an abortion.

Planned Parenthood is one organization that provides health services like birth control and abortions.

This is a way to medically end a pregnancy. Many people see the ruling as a victory for women's rights. They believe it gives women control over their bodies and health.

Abortion rights are still debated today. Many state laws prevent women from getting one if they are more than twenty-four weeks pregnant. Texas passed a law in 2021. It prevented women from getting an abortion if they were more than

THE PILL

The US Food and Drug Administration approved the birth control pill in 1960. The pill helps prevent pregnancy. It let women have more control of their bodies. Before this time, many women had to give up their careers when they became pregnant. The pill helped women have more say in when or if they wanted to start a family.

six weeks pregnant. Many women do not even know they are pregnant at this time.

Many people spoke out against the Texas law. They protested to protect a woman's right to abortion. Hundreds of protests took place all over the country. Still, other states continued to pass restrictive abortion laws. Many people worried the Supreme Court would overturn abortion rights.

WOMEN IN GOVERNMENT

In 2021, there were seventeen countries with female leaders. There is a long way to go before there is gender equality in government. Winnie Byanyima is the director of Oxfam International. This group works to create equality. Byanyima talked about the importance of women in politics. She said, "When you have more women in public decision-making, you get policies that benefit women, children, and families in general." [4]

In 1984, Geraldine Ferraro made US history. She became the first female vice presidential **candidate** for a major US party. She and running mate Walter Mondale lost the election. But she paved the way for future female candidates. Sarah

Hillary Clinton received more than 65 million votes for president in 2016. However, she lost to Donald Trump because he won more electoral votes.

Palin was the vice presidential nominee for the Republican Party in 2008. Hillary Clinton became the presidential nominee for the Democratic Party in 2016. She was the first woman to win a major party's nomination for president. She lost the election to Donald Trump.

Kamala Harris was one of six women who ran for US president in 2020. Kirsten Gillibrand, Amy Klobuchar, and Elizabeth Warren were a few of the other female

SUPPORTING ALL WOMEN

Injustice against women is not limited to women who were assigned female at birth. It is also a problem for **transgender** women. More than 16 percent of trans women experienced domestic violence in 2019. In 2021, US Representatives Ayanna Pressley and Marie Newman introduced a bill to support **LGBTQ** survivors of domestic violence.

candidates. Joe Biden won the Democratic Party presidential nomination. He asked Harris to be his running mate. They won the election. Harris became the first female vice president of the United States. She was also the first Black person and first Indian American to hold the position.

Harris gave a victory speech. She spoke of the many women who had come before her. She thanked them for their roles in advancing gender equality in politics. She said, "I may be the first woman to hold this office. But I won't be the last."[5]

4
ENDING INJUSTICE AGAINST WOMEN

An article about Harvey Weinstein appeared in the *New York Times* in 2017. Weinstein was a successful film producer. The article told the stories of several women who had worked for Weinstein. Some were actors. Others worked behind the camera. The women accused Weinstein of **sexual harassment** and sexual assault. More women came forward with similar stories about Weinstein after the article was published.

The #MeToo movement has raised awareness about sexual assault and harassment around the world.

Lauren O'Connor was one of the women quoted in the article. She had written about Weinstein's behaviors. O'Connor stated, "I am a 28-year-old woman trying to make a living and a career. Harvey Weinstein is a . . . world-famous man, and this is his company. The balance of power is me: 0, Harvey Weinstein: 10."[6] This power imbalance is one reason it can be difficult for survivors to speak out. Men can use their power to abuse women. They use their fame and money to keep survivors silent. Survivors may worry that speaking out will cost them their jobs.

The article sparked the #MeToo movement. People used the hashtag to talk about sexual harassment and assault. People spoke about these issues in entertainment, sports, and politics. Many had been afraid to talk about their

USA GYMNASTICS

Larry Nassar was a doctor for USA Gymnastics for more than thirty years. Former gymnast Rachael Denhollander accused Nassar of sexual assault in 2016. She was the first woman to do so. More than 150 women and girls testified against Nassar. This included several Olympic athletes. Nassar was sentenced in 2018. He faced up to 175 years in prison for abusing his patients.

Brett Kavanaugh was accused of sexual assault in 2018 after being nominated to the US Supreme Court.

experiences. The movement helped people realize they were not alone.

In 2020, a New York court sentenced Weinstein to twenty-three years in prison. Many people saw this as justice. Weinstein was one of many men who have been found guilty of assault or harassment since the #MeToo movement began.

FIGHTING FORCED MARRIAGE

Parents arrange marriages for their grown children in some cultures. Some women have no say in these arrangements. A male family member chooses a husband for his daughter or sister.

In some cases, the bride is still a child. Child brides are separated from their families. They are often victims of abuse. Being married at a young age limits access

Many countries have laws that establish a minimum age for marriage.

to education. It affects job opportunities. Child marriages are most common in South Asia and parts of Africa. About 250 million women worldwide were married before the age of fifteen.

Three Nigerian women want to make child marriage illegal in the country. Kudirat Abiola, Temitayo Asuni, and Susan Ubogu formed the nonprofit organization Never Your Fault. The organization started an online campaign in 2018. It was called Raise the Age. The founders asked the Nigerian government to take a clear stance on child marriage. They called for a ban on marriages for people under eighteen.

The organization also spreads its message through Nigerian communities. Asuni said, "This campaign . . . may have started with an online petition, but the people it affects don't have access to the internet. So, we want to educate them." [7]

THE FIGHT THAT REMAINS

Much progress has been made in fighting injustice against women. But it is an ongoing problem. Women in some countries have limited freedoms. They do not have a choice in what they wear or where they work. Sexual harassment and abuse are other major issues.

Nations can support gender equality by making laws. For example, Iceland requires companies to pay their employees equally.

People in Italy took to the streets on International Women's Day, which occurs annually on March 8.

Nations can also support educational opportunities for girls. Far more girls today receive an education than in the past. About 79 million more girls were enrolled in school in 2020 than in 1998.

Having female leaders in government, such as Kamala Harris, is one step toward ending injustices against women.

Ending injustice against women will take time. It requires hard work. People can call attention to injustices. They can attend protests that raise awareness for women's rights. They can write to lawmakers about important issues. Governments can make laws to create equality. Each step to end injustice can improve the futures of women and girls around the world.

INTERNATIONAL LABOUR ORGANIZATION (ILO)

The ILO is an organization that works to create labor standards. It protects workers. More than 180 countries were part of the ILO in 2022. An ILO treaty came into effect in 2021. It protected people from harassment and violence in the workplace. The treaty stated that people had the right to work in a safe environment. It was the first international treaty to recognize this right.

GLOSSARY

bias

a personal belief or judgment that is often unfair

candidate

someone running for a political office

discrimination

the act of treating people differently based on factors such as race, religion, or gender

jury

a group of people who listen to the evidence of a legal trial and decide whether a person is guilty

LGBTQ

lesbian, gay, bisexual, transgender, and queer

sexual harassment

unwanted physical or verbal behavior that is sexual in nature

suffrage

the right to vote

transgender

relating to a person whose gender identity is different than the sex assigned at birth

SOURCE NOTES

CHAPTER ONE: THE HISTORY OF INJUSTICE AGAINST WOMEN

1. Quoted in Lila Thulin, "Why the Equal Rights Amendment Is Still Not Part of the Constitution," *Smithsonian Magazine*, January 15, 2020. www.smithsonianmag.com.

CHAPTER TWO: INJUSTICE AGAINST WOMEN TODAY

2. Bryan Robinson, "Gender Discrimination Is Still Alive and Well in the Workplace in 2021," *Forbes*, February 15, 2021. www.forbes.com.

3. Quoted in "An Interview About Surviving Human Trafficking: Margeaux Gray," *Office on Women's Health*, October 2, 2016. www.womenshealth.gov.

CHAPTER THREE: KEY MOMENTS IN FIGHTING INJUSTICE AGAINST WOMEN

4. Quoted in Sophie Partridge-Hicks, "5 Ways the World Has Gotten Better for Women & Girls—and 5 Ways It Hasn't," *Global Citizen*, October 6, 2020. www.globalcitizen.org.

5. Quoted in Constance Grady, "Kamala Harris: 'I May Be the First Woman to Hold This Office. But I Won't Be the Last,'" *Vox*, November 7, 2020. www.vox.com.

CHAPTER FOUR: ENDING INJUSTICE AGAINST WOMEN

6. Quoted in Jodi Kantor and Megan Twohey, "Harvey Weinstein Paid Off Sexual Harassment Accusers for Decades," *New York Times*, October 5, 2017. www.nytimes.com.

7. Quoted in Itumeleng Letsoalo, "6 Activists Who Are Fighting Child Marriage in Their Countries," *Global Citizen*, July 10, 2019. www.globalcitizen.org.

FOR FURTHER RESEARCH

BOOKS

Veronica Chambers, *Finish the Fight! The Brave and Revolutionary Women Who Fought for the Right to Vote*. Boston, MA: Versify, 2020.

Tammy Gagne, *Women in the Workplace*. San Diego, CA: ReferencePoint Press, 2019.

Laura K. Murray, *Kamala Harris: First Female US Vice President*. Minneapolis, MN: Abdo Publishing, 2022.

INTERNET SOURCES

Elizabeth Hilfrank, "The Women's Suffrage Movement," *National Geographic*, 2015. https://kids.nationalgeographic.com.

Anna North, "7 Positive Changes that Have Come from the #MeToo Movement," *Vox*, October 4, 2019. www.vox.com.

"Texas Demonstrations Take Aim at State's Near-Total Ban on Abortion," *Texas Tribune*, October 2, 2021. www.texastribune.org.

WEBSITES

American Civil Liberties Union (ACLU)
www.aclu.org/issues/womens-rights

The ACLU was founded in 1920. It strives to protect the rights and freedoms of all individuals.

Oxfam International
www.oxfam.org/en/what-we-do/issues/gender-justice-and-womens-rights

Oxfam International is a global organization that fights inequality. It works to end gender discrimination, poverty, and other injustices.

UN Women
www.unwomen.org/en

UN Women works to protect women around the world. It helps countries set standards for gender equality and end violence against women.

INDEX

abortions, 38–41
Anthony, Susan B., 17–18

Biden, Joe, 45
birth control pills, 40
burqas, 27

child brides, 51–53
Clinton, Hillary, 43–44

domestic abuse, 33, 51, 54

Eastman, Crystal, 21
Equal Pay Act, 30–31
Equal Rights Amendment (ERA), 21–23

Ferraro, Geraldine, 42

gender pay gap, 11, 29–32

Harris, Kamala, 44–45
human trafficking, 33–35

juries, 18–21

#MeToo Movement, 49–51
Mott, Lucretia, 17, 21

Never Your Fault, 53
Nineteenth Amendment, 18, 36

Palin, Sarah, 42–43
Paul, Alice, 21

Roe v. Wade, 38–39

Seneca Falls, 16
sexual harassment, 47, 49, 51, 54, 57
Stanton, Elizabeth Cady, 17–18

Taliban, 6–9, 24–29
transgender women, 44
Trump, Donald, 37–38, 44

US Constitution, 18–19, 22–23, 36
US Supreme Court, 20–21, 38, 41

voting, 11, 15–16, 18

Weinstein, Harvey, 46–48, 50
Wells-Barnett, Ida B., 17
Women's March, 38
women's suffrage movement, 16–18, 36

Yousafzai, Malala, 6–9

IMAGE CREDITS

Cover: © Peace Portal Photo/Alamy
5: © Sheila Fitzgerald/Shutterstock Images
7: © SN 040288/Shutterstock Images
8: © Pradeep Gaurs/Shutterstock Images
10: © bizoo_n/iStockphoto
13: © Rieke Photos/Shutterstock Images
14: Currier & Ives/Library of Congress/Journal of the American Revolution/Wikimedia
16: Rice & Brady/Library of Congress
19: © Sir Travel A Lot/Shutterstock Images
22: National Photo Company Collection/Library of Congress
25: © solmaz daryani/Shutterstock Images
26: © Rido/Shutterstock Images
31: © Red Line Editorial
34: © John Gomez/Shutterstock Images
37: © Michael Candelori/Shutterstock Images
39: © EPG Euro Photo Graphics/Shutterstock Images
43: © Rebekah Zemansky/Shutterstock Images
47: © Julian Leshay/Shutterstock Images
50: © Rachael Warriner/Shutterstock Images
52: © Stephen Coburn/Shutterstock Images
55: © Good Life Studio/iStockphoto
56: © BiksuTong/Shutterstock Images

ABOUT THE AUTHOR

Tammy Gagne has written hundreds of books for both adults and children. Some of her recent books have been about gender dysphoria and women in the workplace. She lives in northern New England with her husband, son, and dogs.